Printed in the United States of America

ISBN: 9798697533444

Book design: Jenna M. Cavanaugh

First Edition 2020

notes to self

a collection of learnings

for the women who inspired these stories
for the men who view them as equals

on the self

I am still learning to nurture
The map of stretch marks that hug
My silhouetted hourglass skin
Fatty gravel roads looping around
Bulging hips that sway a little too much
Freckle constellations // an entire sky
Bird nests of blue veins and brown patches
A stiff-lined nose too similar to my mother's
Two hazels that stare back at the reflection

that we are so capable of filling others with love
yet so often fail at reciprocating it to ourselves

– the relationship with the self can be the most toxic

drape the dirty laundry over the clothesline
right there on the front lawn as they drive by
and stare –

how we create a habit of confusing masked flaws
with achieved perfection

I have a really-that's-your-issue problem
Because really, it is my issue,
And really, I wish it wasn't.
Crumpled-bags-in-the-passenger-seat
Stale-fried-smell-actually-make-it-a-large
Find-a-trash-can-to-throw-out-the-regret
Problem.
Swallow my insecurities whole.
Take a fork and dig in.
Don't cry –
Eat.

remove *fine* from a person's vocabulary
& watch what rawness unravels

The world was a snow globe for the first time that season.
In all those wrinkled sheets in unfamiliar apartments
with lukewarm showers and new flavors of peppermint breath,
I was aching to feel wanted, be wanted, first and foremost,
before all other pretty girls with pretty, pink lips in pretty skirts
that hit above pretty knees because they're pretty –
p e r f e c t,
and that's what pretty girls do.
It was growing colder outside, and so was I.
I had ripped through wrinkled sheets in unfamiliar apartments
searching for the desire to feel wanted, be wanted,
first and foremost,
before all other pretty girls.
The snow began to quietly settle.
My insides were scraped clean at my feet.

Oh darling, don't you see?
Look up, come closer, dear.
It is time to feel wanted, be wanted,
first and foremost,
by yourself.

you were that firework kind of being
the type that loves to be almost
too much until it's just the right amount
of pretty sparkling to draw a crowd —
crackle and sizzle and set fire to yourself
the kind of magic so goddamn ironic
living in a tender balance of ego and selflessness
they can't help but stare

what ultimate tragedy to light up so bright
only to end up sacrificing yourself when
the world fades to a quiet, lonely dark

today, it has been decided that
sensitivity is not a weakness

for wielding the ability to empathize
heals more than frigid ever could.

to be woman
is to hold everything
the world tells you to be
then stare them back
in the whites of their eyes
when you decide differently

femininity looks a lot like pink on the billboards,
but being a woman is built on so many things
// that aren't plastic \\

Sometimes,
  I like to trace my stretch marks with my fingers;
violent purple, warm red,
  and a fading, murky white
paint these bold hips and a swinging stomach --
  craters upon the surface of my skin moon.

the greatest fuel for a strong-minded woman
is being told she *cannot*

could never

oh?

just watch me.

a collection of humid Sundays:
listen closely for the laughter –
fragile questions // heavy thinking
of tomorrow and the next
year
or many more after
but they take a sip of wine and forget about that for awhile

because today, they're
summer-feet-propped-up-
excited-candles-and-a-lot-of-unknowns

but they hold hands for a minute now
before their minds take off for the stars
breathe out the smoke slowly
one song she can't help but sing along to

they feel it all together
staring back at an entire world right underneath their toes

Grey Saturday mornings are sometimes best suited alone.

I lost that voice somewhere between summer and
autumn; she used to tell and tell me *keep loving,*

but doubt came screaming to corrode my eardrums.
A mob of strangers outside my bedroom window:

you are not worth it because you never were,
they would say in loud whispers, and I listened.

It takes a special kind of Saturday morning before
the world sirens and bursts on our doorstep.

I held my soft stomach bulging onto the bedsheets;
let's begin to love you like I did once again.

Self-worth is not a destination or a checklist;
it is, every day, choosing yourself – despite of –

not always because of.

When it all becomes too heavy, resting is not weakness;
it is merely the time spent regaining the strength needed
to carry it all once again.

& those
therapy-kind-of car rides
to therapy-type-of places
where a bleeding sunset
fixes a soul like it does when
i catch your face crack slowly
into that sunrise-kind-of smile

it was in the moment she realized
he could take nothing more from her,

that she was finally free.

I'll be here chasing the stoplight reflections
On city pavement right after a rainstorm,
But something about the painted yellow lines
Reminds me of a backroad that loops around
A nestled farmhouse tucked on a corner lot.
Rummage through piles of worn photographs
In boxes with the sports trophies / art class clay sculptures.

No matter the ferocious hunger for new, pretty places,
Returning to my hometown will always feel like going home.

When they begin the comparisons,
I jump to say I have your stubbornness //
your grit // your poise.

Admiration seeps in many forms,
and this, in fate, is mine.

– my father's daughter

change always seemed so discomforting,
but then again, her favorite season was full of it.

– autumn

Words are the thoughts we write into the world with Sharpie,
so while they barrel rotted hate with bullets and drones,
I think about the unmatched power behind speaking freely.
Without wound \ stitch \ casket arrangement,
free speech might be the most precious weapon we hold
that leaves behind impact and impression instead of scars.

on the scars

I've always had a thing for scars
& messy stories.

Boys learn that girls like it rough
When he pushes her into the wood chips
On the playground.
The stinging and dripping are overshadowed
By his thick, persuasive smile,
And that is the first time she will confuse
Pain with flirtation.

This is not a summer love story,
And I will not aerate every detail
Of her thirty-rack-backyard-Sleepy-Blue-Eyed-Boy-come-let-
me-show-you-his-hand-her-skirt-shiver-nails-digging-bend-
her-over-the-railing-dry-fuck-screaming-lullaby-shhhh-it's-
their-secret;
This is how her innocence cracks, bent over
Behind a shed to a Sleepy Blue-Eyed Boy,
And that is the first time she will confuse
Insistence with sensuality.

And there will be more first times
When a woman has no chessboard move left
Other than to confuse truth with lie
Because it is her word against a
Patriarchy that does a damn good job
At keeping its walls too high to climb.

She strides up to the wall and decides
Today is no day for climbing.
Pull out one brick – slowly. Be careful,
Be thorough.
The ground underneath quakes.
The walls begin to crumble.
One foot forward, then the other,
Leaving Sleepy Blue-Eyed Boy behind in
A thickening cloud of dust,
She marches through.

Those marks carved onto your chest
Sure look like her and her too,
And I bet all your girls twist their promises
Like cherry stems against plump lips,
So when I arrive, why should you believe me?

My hair is not glittering sunshine.
My skeletons don't hide behind my lashes.
These are not the only ways that I'm different from them.

never had she ever //
heartstrings made of leather

It was a Tuesday when
my coffee was just warm
enough but not really
strong enough to satisfy.
You appeared in the
store window with that
reckless, lazy look about you.

I won't ask how your mother is
because you pushed off telling her,
didn't you?
You are no longer through the
window blowing up a balloon
in my tired chest,
and on second thought,
tell you mother I say hi.

for all the times we cut lips with words
instead of holding you up –

the immeasurable sacrifice to love like a mother

& the first thing I thought of –
        Not that fight or a stifled quiet room –
Your voice melting the shaky candles.

I was rocked to sleep by Petty
        Or the Keys or some other kind of
Spiritual rock n' roll that made her feel –

Dear Mama,
        I'm calling from underwater,
And the signal doesn't seem to be working.

The tide is coming in now,
        And they came crawling for my beating chest.
I don't really know what or where to go,

And all I can keep thinking of is the last –
        Give me a minute before I can finish a sentence
Because full inhales are running with the tide.

What I'd really rather is crawl out of my body and to you
        Wherever that might be – I think the stars
Tucked all pretty above our heads

Like her eyes and side smile on a soft Tuesday.
        I think that's where she is,
And on a night as shaky and dark as this.

The first thing I thought of – the very first thing –
        Is a shining star that looks a lot like me, her, him;
Mama, it looks so much like you.

I knew I'd miss you something awful
When the leaves changed.

But don't mistake me,
This is not a love poem.

This is only to say we were right,
And it sits heavy
On a heart that still falls in rhythm
With the sound of a crackling radio
On an early morning drive.

& when the dust settles //

when ring lines on fingers begin to show,

my biggest heartbreak will reflect

in unsettling warm, brown eyes

between a sharp nose and summer hair like our mother's.

these boys can chew on my heartstrings

and laugh between my legs, but darling,

nothing compares to the shatter of the one

who shares those sticky summers and picture frames.

give me the growls from hungry hyena women

and late-night alleyway creatures out for blood

before tainting my own with cold shoulders

and a string of unanswered calls.

for a girl like me has an appetite for challenge,

and a ferocious attraction to the difficult,

cycling life's phases to find a type of love-you-too fading

with the sunrise in unsettling warm, brown eyes

      between a sharp nose and summer hair very much

like our mother's.

I can't blame you for hating me.
My temper gets too hot to the touch
Leaving behind blisters that turn to scars.

A reputation of reds and purples,
And all I came here to say
Is just like you –
I hate that part of me, too.

for my chest can spark wildfires
& ashes always made for a messy cleanup

Currently reconciling
A shelled scorpion
With a rose petal.

Stinging or wilting,
Aggressive and fragile:

When you ask who I am, and I reply,
"A walking contradiction,"
This is your answer, my dear:

Sometimes petal // sometimes scorpion.
Gentle enough to break, but
Difficult enough to seethe venom.

iMillennials

welcome to the age of attention addiction
// so shoot me up with a
like-love-double-tap-lit-up-screen-for-bedtime-stories-no-
answer-next-option-as-Band-Aids
tell all of them *you're the very only* (maybe one will bend)
ratio-status-as-class-too-much-or-perfect-filter-the-mistakes-as-
highlights-reeling-this-is-my-angle-not-yours

Read 1:06 AM

a generation of a lot of things,
and one of them is cold.

people are not meant to be like items
we entertainingly move in-and-out of
online shopping carts in a game of boredom
waiting for a discount – "Place Order"

– commodifying human beings

Pick up my feet, callused and worn and, well, a little tired.
Find slices on the bottoms where the eggshells cut the surface.

Sneaking a signal up to where you are in the clouds
To tell you rushing over robin baby blues leaves marks

That sting under hot water, but scalding is the temperature
That will remind my toes that they can wiggle to regain feeling.

Good things fall apart // good people surely do.
Treat my body with your curious, your jigsaw puzzle & tell me,

Were you going to take-it-thief-it-in-the-night with my –
Slip-in-slip-out when no one worthwhile was watching?

Call me beautiful \ crazy / something to relax my limbs.
Pull for the one thing that all others couldn't quite reach.

I stayed to watch you finish putting together my pieces because
Warmth tends to overtake logic for doe-eyed, too-young things.

Dancing on eggshells that turned robin baby blue to red –
"No" was enough, so I guess I came here to thank you.

you did not want her
how she asked to be wanted,
so let her go.

– what's deserved

Listen when I say
That boy is fine without you,
So you will be, too.

the curve of her hips reminds you of me
in an early dawn light.
kiss her collarbone once more –
avoid the eyes, for that's the giveaway:

hers warm like sun rays;
mine set your skin on fire.

humanity's worst habit
is to break the things we love
before they get a chance
to break us first

— self-preservation

bury the answers in a corner with the clichés
"it'll all work out" because "everything happens for a reason"
when you felt it, was it butterflies?
or more like a scorpion's sting – slow and certain

"it gets better with time" is never convincing
at the moment when it's said
because the wounds are still split open
and no time has passed to help the healing

"you'll just know"s from those who believe they do –
so before it comes spilling and crawling,
take it as a friendly reminder that some advice
fills spaces like drugstore party balloons:

thin in material // simply full of air

jenna m. cavanaugh

tell it once
show it twice
for anything else
sits cold as ice

She had blindly fallen for all of the futures
with her fabrications,
sculpting boys with her fantasies
like Play-Doh,
leaving aside their real shells
discarded on the pavement.

I know a boy who wasn't ever mine to keep.
Summer slipped between my fingers
& we rolled the die on creaky floors,
Playing games while batting lashes.

I asked you to take all that I could give
On a sweating summer night almost
Too tucked away from the stars
In some unfamiliar tangled spaces.

There was a part of you broken off jagged,
Lying in another bed in another town.
There was a part of me shattered fragile
Hung up on him like a stale winter coat.

How delicate a thing to hold onto someone
Just simply for what they are in the now
Before life's great perhaps wiggles in
With jaded logic to dirty a daydream.

feeling what it could be
knowing that it isn't

- the butter/lies

there's no persistence medal awarded
for forcing someone to stay

I'm owed an apology
I'll never receive.
I owe somebody else an apology
I'll never mature enough to make.

And that's how life works, doesn't it:
We fuck up and grow up.
Fuck up then grow up.

I don't wish you the best, I wish you a life
Greater than what we could've ever dreamed
That morning when the sun rose,
Peeking through wheat stalks and grass blades
Reflecting off foggy car windows and billows of smoke,
And I left, and you knew better than to ask me to stay.
I wish you a life greater than the magic
Of moments like that.

This is how the curtain closes:
Quiet but loud in thought —
Unnoticeable except for those who are watching.

& they'll linger somewhere between
crustless sandwiches
and a stale sort of affection
quite often confused with love

when you miss someone,
it comes in waves:
riptides after midnight
& ocean depths during
midday grocery store runs.

there is no precise finality
to walking off heartbreak;
no point when it's over:
a tear allotment reached
like a cycle of laundry.

moving on from someone
isn't quick and simple.
it gets better, then it comes
crashing at the sight of a
book or smell or song.

*I thought it was you
standing in the coffee shop
like that one grey morning
you ordered coffee black
while I was free falling.*

the things* that cannot be diagnosed and healed
with prescriptions in labeled orange bottles
are the things that leave us so lost while we look
for the answers that don't even exist to be found

  *there isn't a cure for loneliness

we rang in this one like the irony was inevitable.
stiff, cold air left slices on our doorsteps, but inside,
champagne flowed and rosy cheeks warmed the walls.

she drifted to sleep and woke up smiling at the thought of
him thinking of her across the city lights at midnight.
all was calm and all was bright and all was untouched.

3...

they arrived with bulldozers to change the pretty narrative
we had begun because how can you believe in anything good
when everything bad bleeds through our phone speakers.

when what was never meant to break doesn't snap, it crumbles.
leaders spitting blood of the Black men they watched lay
suffering on pavement while declaring STATUS QUO 2020.

2...

when masses of masks replaced the standard sidewalk etiquette
of uncomfortably polite smiles and quick head nods:
a Silicon Valley kingdom to have our technology control.

outside these walls, the world lay in a state of unprecedented
like that last night we stared through the gold beads
with a big breath in pause and fingers crossed behind backs.

1...

// Wherever you are,
I hope that everything
That once hurt enough
To leave it all behind,
And me here with it,
Is finally, finally gone. \\

on the outside

how many times have you been in love, my dear?

& all that comes rushing are egg-yolk sunrises
against jade back arches of the lazy River Seine
greasy saxophones and piano notes tripping up
cobblestone stairs on the street corners

oh, tellement de fois, ma chérie –

for she had fallen for so many city heartbeats
warmly tucked between river & skyline in distant places

music brings to life the type of invisible web
that pulls together a room full of strangers as the

// lights
        // go
                // down

((art is healing))

I've found that midnights in strange places
hold an invincible kind of magic.

Look at those pretty city veins
Glittering from far below
>> *// Where do you think that one is going?*

Maybe Europe, oh I hope it's Paris
With a tower that sparkles
To outshine lights in other places

Flirting & curtsying &
Winking at the sky
>> *// My goodness, will you look at that*

Come down a bit now to fall
Into the clouds – let's jump
& float down slowly

Dot cars & cardboard homes
>> *// Let's play House and pretend*
Just for a little while

Perspective adjustments
From tiny window-seat travel
& She boasts & bubbles of

>> // City veins

>> // Cardboard places

the purple mountains are there to remind hungry humans
that, in a great perspective, we are still so very small.

so when we arrive at the site with bulldozers and chains,
forcing the purple mountains to fall, so will we.

– Mother Nature is a mother // love her like one

in a world birthed from space rock,
boasting burnt red desert cliffs //
thickly humid, green jungle leaves,
why is it so difficult for those living
on a landscape built and bred in diversity
to feel the same about each other, too?

– A (P)lanet (O)f (C)olor

a west coast set to burn in a
grim fairytale where the dragon
wins // spilling smoke from its
nostrils and igniting the ground below

an east coast now up in flames from
autumn's colors bursting on treetops –
deep, velvet reds // smoldering orange
flickers of golden on each stem

coast to coast // fire to ashes
when they say nothing's changed
& we will be forever invincible
point them in the direction of the

// dust piles

Men and girls came and went between rows of clean hedges
Tucked in turquoise gardens hugging foaming seas
Creaking porch chairs that rock, rock, rock
Lackadaisically in a sigh of salty breeze
No socks needed for summer feet dangled
Off the back of sleek yacht hulls or tucked
In loafers from Thursdays in the pretty city
Is she born with it, or is it the checkbook-paper-cuts-
Lilly-patterned-heartaches-*I-thought-the-gardener-*
Knew-to-trim-these-Nantucket-Red-faced-scotch-
And-rosé-scandal-white-and-white-and-white-
And –
Isn't this better than the Disney version?
An island town with properties oozing hydrangeas
Mr. Presidents vacation here you know
Lululemon water for Saturday morning jogs
Avocado toast, but it'll cost her an arm and a
Bentley –
Daddy, money doesn't grow on trees
But it sure looks good with Edgartown Green
For a Vineyard Gatsby always knows how to
Match his net worth with a damn good tie

a simple, little things era
when a whole world was told
"no"
even those who weren't used
to following the rules

streets scattered empty &
money can buy just about
anything
and everything besides a life
or a do-over when the opponent

is God – religion isn't my
kind of therapy or solace
yet
what other choice did we have
when it was us against the

infinite
unknown?

it's between the static noise // bylines
exposed grainy cellphone footage
that America is once again reminded
our rooted problems don't disintegrate
when bigger demons come knocking

seas of masked faces // closed doors
but mouths that cannot be taped
& we repeat the strange fruit
that those who let hate rot within steep
to continue to bear and to nurture

running shoes tucked by the door —
I wonder why we continue to confuse
daily privileges like exercise and school
with a hot-bellied systemic violence
that loyally returns to wait, mouth foaming
outside on our own stoops and staircases

Today, my life will not change
for I am swaddled in white satin privilege –
white satin and White Houses and white marble
cold under your feet.

Look at me. You see a girl.
Look at you. I see cracks.

a whole nation weakened
& it's a struggle
to digest that a life
is the compensation we
pay for demanded justice

((almost nine minutes under a riptide))
I'd like to believe it's against
the compassion that makes us
simply h u m a n
to ignore sounds seeking help
before the drowning

i c a n t b r e a t h e

drowning under weights of headlines
loud voices over television screens
murmurs and quick whispers and
slow sighs — the kind that bite in stiff air

while we're troubled in the meantime
let's daydream about those clouds

we'll meet on the other side
to make tonight or tomorrow
or maybe next week, too —
a little softer
a little kinder
a little more temporary

it takes feeling the empathy ingrained in human beings

to outweigh our animalistic instinct that screams
just protect yourself

// realize we are lucky to be born capable of compassion

& it takes a fool content to fall back on his heels in a past time

to not take advantage of our superpower

((we were made to care and therefore are responsible to do so))

they say
you are the company you keep

well let that apply to newsfeeds
// live streams // replyretweetrepost
it starts only looking like our own opinions
social media mirroring scrolls on
the face of a lit-up phone screen

so before we ask how could he
                              dare she
believe in ——————————

we are the company we keep
and our mirrors hold different pictures

so let it take the courage to be quite
u n c o m f o r t a b l e to make room
for seeing other people's reflections

valuing human beings equally
is not a topic up for discussion —
it's not an opinion. it's not a feeling.

like a paper cut,
quick & slicing,
it's that simple.

that we're granted a voice
but choose to cut our words with hate

— speak wisely

When the world becomes a bit too much to lean on,
let's go to that grassy knoll in Vermont:
the one a sharp walk up the hill near the maple
syrup farm with wild daises and lavender.

Let's play on dirtied floors between aged arcade games
in the little red silo between mountaintops.
Take me to the gurgling creek where he skinned his
knee against mossy rocks. You picked him up
while quiet whimpers slowly grew to a cry.

I find my daydreams tangle between sharp cheddar
samples and thick fudge from the country store
because nostalgia tastes as temporary as spilling water.

I love you like I did back then long before the
"what if"'s and outgrown lullabies,

so if you find your mind wandering to the spot we
chased stars, meet me in Vermont where a little girl

in blue overalls floats on the wheat stalks singing
Tracy Chapman records until dawn.

on the warmth

Tapping raindrops on the rooftop.
Steaming coffee mugs in bed.

Ice cream sundaes for dinner.
2 A.M. diner-booth breakfast sandwiches.

Sandy feet dangled out of the passenger side.
Nerves tucked behind blushing dimples.

– the simple, little things

You call on the way home.
You don't say you miss her,
    But instead, a diatribe of
        Alternate routes and workarounds
          To avoid 95
Serves as a sticky sweet stand-in
For it'd get her home faster
    And closer to you.

Keep loving her;
It reminds her of dried flowers,
    Warm blankets,
        The sharp whistled "s" sounds,
          A pair of doughy blue eyes;
It reminds me of you.

oh tenacious, little bird,
through all the nesting,
you never fail to return home
to ensure that we're warm

– JoAnne

choosing the ones you call home
back and forth and over again

– family is built on friendships, too.

we don't talk enough about the kind of relationships between
friends:
the "I love you"s curled up on bathroom floors or 4 A.M. glue
drying
as we put each other's pieces back together in comfortable
silence.
some can span over decades even before the twentysomething
blues
come crashing down between old photographs holding onto old
beginnings.

it's the effort put in between moving boxes and brand-new
floors
because we spend so much time trying to keep dating who we
date
that sometimes we forget there are ones who already love us
for us;
finish our sentence or story about that one time that one wild
night.

relationships between women,
        the friendship kind,
             the true love kind,
                  are magic.

sisterhood can live outside of a bloodline
in file cabinets of uncontrollable laughter
making tear rivers or sibling face-offs at dark

we laid head-to-head under a blanket of
glowing stars, and I thanked one that twinkled
back for handing down a sister for me to love
as well as a friend –

(opposites that, together, make us whole just the same)

if they were ever to open you up,
they'd find a bright light illuminating your chest
for it's what makes them stare a second too long
you, my dear friend, capture the throats in the room

a twinkling laugh that makes the trees bend to listen
tangled piles of colored yarn for veins
stained, parted lips like your mother's
jade stones for eyes like your grandfather's

for a woman as spectacular as that
needs no preface or foreword
she can't help but glint and bounce like rays
when they catch a mirror piece just right

old friendships are the most comforting reminder
that who you were and who you've become
are equally worthy of a love that stays

we're just friends
        // until it was more
                // soon-to-be everything

There was always a slight mischief in the way she pulled her
lip before a retort.

& just like that,
He knew He was one step into a hurricane.

She fell for the way
he smiled with his eyes —

it was a wicked little
trick, like smoke & Cabernet
on an overcast Sunday,
and not for the world would She
give it back.

I was never good at asking for help,
but I'll fight your dragons
and make a millennial out of
any outdated Cinderella story.

Your mouth dripped honey.
The bees buzzing told me to take shelter, but
my heart: *enjoy the nectar.*

Suddenly, I developed a sweet tooth.

tongue tasting smoky breath //
cheeks grazing rough stubble

warm eyes say Nice Guy
hair pulls say otherwise

I don't need whiskey on ice
when I crave something that bites like this

I tickle your ear with
Please play me.

Placed tongue on the mouthpiece
Quick fingers lead up a crescendo
Hold up the chorus a moment longer
& make me sing for you.

((I always did love this song.))

Baby, if a moment like that
isn't made for Hollywood lights,

it'll sure make for one hell of a poem.

11:11s and melting birthday candles

My thumb scooped up your eyelash.
Your breath tickled my finger,
And I made one too.

I wished for you.

She could be anything in this world
& what she wanted was to be his.

((my religion))

I don't pray to one Almighty Power
or an Ultimate Kingdom to cross into.

I don't find solace in the unexplainable,
but, my dear, this I believe is true:

Something out there brought me to here,
and for that, my faith is in you.

smiling into my steering wheel –
that's when I knew

// you

// had

// me

all of the whispers passed between touched noses
from slept-in beds on lazy, drooping Sundays
giggled flirtations spouting from bodies

the slow kiss you feel buzzing through your toes
electric zaps from fingers roaming between legs
and slated among *we got carried away* are

i don't really tell many people that pillow
secrets that will remain tucked in the sheets
because bedrooms on lazy, drooping Sundays

are special, hidden places – far from the outside
in all of their passionate convictions, but merely a
few paces behind any cold stoop and front door

a honeycomb laugh like your mother's
but a side smile so much like your father's

((the parts of you she fell for first))

fitting like puzzle pieces
forgetting about the rest

– the warmth

As we replace the type of warmth
that only comes from tangled limbs // full hearts
with nights of lingering self doubt & empty spaces,
I want to thank you for that moment
you made me feel tall enough to hug the clouds;
Eyes that kept on me during my travels to the sky,
Or when my skin melted into yours like that bottle of red.
I fell asleep in your clothes to draw you in from miles away
pretending to be something greater, something very much like
yours.

We crossed lifetime zones to hold hands,
and I might've started our chapter deeper in a notebook –
fate might've fucked with the timing, darling,
but sometimes on an overcast daydreaming Wednesday,
I like to think of your scrunched face during a full-belly laugh
and smile.

I remembered what it felt like to fall
and disregard what the ground looks like
on my way down from the stars.

My dreams can play tricks
where I find myself twirling
between bookshelves or
squinting at a burning sunrise.

When it's a kiss,
(I mean a really good one),
I begin to lose feeling like
the pause on a television screen.

It's like the mind already knows
that the end is inevitable,
so in the meantime,
life moves in slow motion.

For all a girl like me hopes for,
with a heart cranked open
on her dress sleeve,
is a kiss,

(I mean a really good one).
The type that causes the
world to get real quiet while
the outside rolls right on by.

I don't know love like they do,
but, because of you, I know the fall.

– what we remember

\\

how beautiful to know that you are still capable of love
amidst all that fights it in our state of unprecedented

//

Acknowledgments

a writer's inspiration is made up of all that surrounds her –
to the family / friends / once-strangers who are part of this story
((to the greatest support system a girl could ever ask for))

– thank you

www.ingramcontent.com/pod-product-compliance
Lightning Source LLC
Chambersburg PA
CBHW071916120726
48001CB00005B/1757